History Highlights

TIMELINE *of the* MUSLIM WORLD

By Charlie Samuels

Gareth Stevens
Publishing

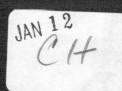

Please visit our Web site www.garethstevens.com. For a free color catalog of all our high-quality books, call toll free 1-800-542-2595 or fax 1-877-542-2596.

Library of Congress Cataloging-in-Publication Data
Samuels, Charlie, 1961-
    Timeline of the Muslim world / Charlie Samuels.
        p. cm. — (History highlights)
    Includes index.
    ISBN 978-1-4339-3489-6 (library binding)
    ISBN 978-1-4339-3490-2 (pbk.)
    ISBN 978-1-4339-3491-9 (6-pack.)
    1. Civilization, Islamic—Juvenile literature. 2. Islamic countries—History—Juvenile literature.
    3. Islam—History—Juvenile literature. I. Title.
    DS36.85.S26 2010
    909'.09767—dc22   2009041579

Published in 2010 by
Gareth Stevens Publishing
111 East 14th Street, Suite 349
New York, NY 10003

© 2010 The Brown Reference Group Ltd.

For Gareth Stevens Publishing:
Art Direction: Haley Harasymiw
Editorial Direction: Kerri O'Donnell

For The Brown Reference Group Ltd:
Editorial Director: Lindsey Lowe
Managing Editor: Tim Cooke
Editor: Ben Hollingum
Children's Publisher: Anne O'Daly
Design Manager: David Poole
Designer: Karen Perry
Picture Manager: Sophie Mortimer
Production Director: Alastair Gourlay

Picture Credits:
Front Cover: Jupiter Images: Photos.com:

Corbis: Paul Almasy: 14; Lebrecht: 31; Christine Osborne: 29; The Picture Desk: 26; Ruggero Vanni: 17; Roger Wood: 16; istockphoto: 6, 7, 9b, 10, 11b, 12t, 20t, 21, 22, 23, 25, 32t, 34,, 35b, 36, 37, 38, 41t, 42, 44, 45; Hulton Archive: 20b, 40b; Jupiter Images: Photos.com: 9t, 18, 28, 32b, 39; Stockxpert: 5, 7b, 13, 41b; Shutterstock: 30; Ettore Emanuele Fanciulli: 33, Adam Przezak: 12b

All Artworks Brown Reference Group

Publisher's note to educators and parents: Our editors have carefully reviewed the Web sites that appear on p. 47 to ensure that they are suitable for students. Many Web sites change frequently, however, and we cannot guarantee that a site's future contents will continue to meet our high standards of quality and educational value. Be advised that students should be closely supervised whenever they access the Internet.

Manufactured in the United States of America
1 2 3 4 5 6 7 8 9 12 11 10

CPSIA compliance information: Batch #BRW0102GS: For further information contact Gareth Stevens, New York, New York at 1-800-542-2595.

Contents

Introduction

Today Islam is followed by more than one in five of the global population. This book traces the remarkable rise of the religion from its origins among nomadic Arab tribes.

Within only a few decades of the death of the Prophet Muhammad in A.D. 632 , the religion he founded had come to dominate the Arabian Peninsula. Arab warriors went on to carry Islam into west Asia, from where it spread east to Persia, central Asia, and the Indian subcontinent; they carried it west to Egypt, from where it spread through North Africa and into the Iberian Peninsula of Europe. The spread of the religion brought cultural unity to many different societies. From the cities of west Africa to the steppes of central Asia, Islam inspired a flowering in the arts, sciences, and religious scholarship.

Division and Conflict

At the same time as it was a highly dynamic faith, Islam was also deeply divided. Conflicts about who should follow Muhammad as the religion's leader caused a bitter split between two branches of Muslims, Sunnis and Shiites. The division still causes conflict today. Meanwhile, powerful dynasties dominated the Muslim world at different periods. They included the Arab Abbasids, the Egyptian Mamelukes, the Persian Safavids, and the Turkic Seljuks and Ottomans. Muslim empires also clashed with their neighbors, particularly the Christians of Europe.

About This Book

This book focuses on the first thousand years of Islamic history, from about 600 to 1600. It contains two different types of timelines. Along the bottom of the pages is a timeline that covers the whole period. It lists key events and developments, color-coded by region. Each chapter also has its own timeline, running vertically down the sides of the pages. This timeline provides more specific details about the particular subject of the chapter.

The Dome of the Rock in Jerusalem is one of the world's oldest mosques, built by Arab invaders in 692. ↓

Muhammad and Islam

One of the world's great religions emerged in the Arabian Peninsula. One man, the Prophet Muhammad, gave the Arabs first a spiritual and then a military mission.

The Kaaba, or black stone, was a holy site for Arabs before the birth of Islam. »

TIMELINE
600–650

KEY:

EUROPE

ASIA

AFRICA

606 Harshavardhana begins to build a large Buddhist empire in north and east India.

622 A defeat by the Byzantines marks the start of the decline of the Sassanian Empire.

614 Sassanians from Persia capture Jerusalem.

622 Muhammad and his followers flee from Mecca to Medina; this Hijra, or flight, marks the start of the Muslim calendar.

600   610   620

c.570 The Prophet Muhammad is born in Mecca, Arabia.

c.610 The archangel Gabriel first appears to Muhammad.

622 The Hijra, or "emigration": Muhammad and his followers leave Mecca for Medina. The Hijra marks the start of the Muslim calendar.

627 A Meccan army is turned back from Medina at the Battle of the Ditch.

630 Mecca surrenders to the Muslims. Muhammad raids north to the borders of Byzantine Syria.

632 Muhammad dies. Elders elect his father-in-law, Abu Bakr, to inherit his authority as khalifah, or caliph ("successor"),

↑ The teachings of Muhammad are recorded in Islam's holy book, the Qur'an.

The Arabs' lifestyle as nomadic camel herders was adapted to one of the world's most hostile environments. To the east the Iran-based empire of the Sassanians flourished. To the north were the Greco-Roman realms of Byzantium. The Arabs stood apart, as though history had passed them by.

Visions of God

All this would change, however, when in 610 a middle-aged businessman in the city of Mecca started seeing visions.

← Muslims learn to recite the Qur'an as part of everyday worship.

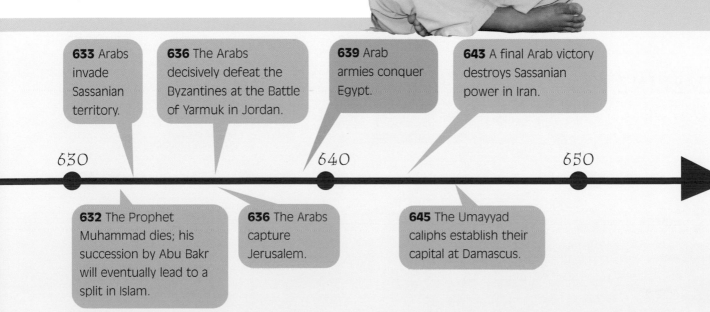

633 Arabs invade Sassanian territory.

636 The Arabs decisively defeat the Byzantines at the Battle of Yarmuk in Jordan.

639 Arab armies conquer Egypt.

643 A final Arab victory destroys Sassanian power in Iran.

630

640

650

632 The Prophet Muhammad dies; his succession by Abu Bakr will eventually lead to a split in Islam.

636 The Arabs capture Jerusalem.

645 The Umayyad caliphs establish their capital at Damascus.

rather than his son-in-law Ali, with huge implications for Islamic history.

636 Victory at the Yarmuk River brings Byzantine Syria under Muslim control.

637 Victory over Persia at the Battle of Qadisiya opens the way to Iraq and Iran.

641 The Arabs take Cairo, Egypt.

644 Caliph Umar is assassinated. His successor, Uthman, gathers Muhammad's teachings into into a single book, the Qur'an.

From a heartland near the Red Sea, Islam first spread over the Arabian Peninusula, then the Near East. →

In the years that followed, the archangel Gabriel appeared to Muhammad again and again, dictating to him the word of Allah—God. The name for the new religion, Islam, meant "surrender" to the divine will.

Inspired by religious zeal and a message of charity for the poor, Muhammad and his followers were at odds with the Quraysh, Mecca's wealthy elite. In 622, they left for the neighboring city of Medina. Relations with Medina's three tribes of Jews were good at first, although as hostilities with Mecca escalated, they deteriorated.

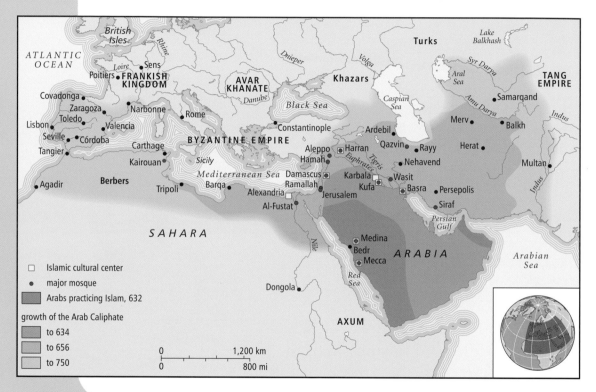

Key:
- □ Islamic cultural center
- • major mosque
- Arabs practicing Islam, 632
- growth of the Arab Caliphate
  - to 634
  - to 656
  - to 750

0 — 1,200 km
0 — 800 mi

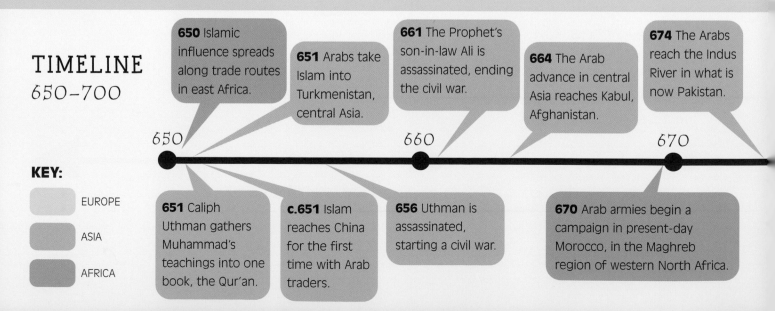

TIMELINE
650–700

650 Islamic influence spreads along trade routes in east Africa.

651 Arabs take Islam into Turkmenistan, central Asia.

661 The Prophet's son-in-law Ali is assassinated, ending the civil war.

664 The Arab advance in central Asia reaches Kabul, Afghanistan.

674 The Arabs reach the Indus River in what is now Pakistan.

650   660   670

651 Caliph Uthman gathers Muhammad's teachings into one book, the Qur'an.

c.651 Islam reaches China for the first time with Arab traders.

656 Uthman is assassinated, starting a civil war.

670 Arab armies begin a campaign in present-day Morocco, in the Maghreb region of western North Africa.

KEY:
- EUROPE
- ASIA
- AFRICA

← Pilgrims pray at the mosque in Mecca in this illustration from an old Persian book.

In time, the Muslims gained control of Mecca, and their victory marked the start of one of the most amazing campaigns of conquest the world has seen. By the time the Prophet died in 632, to be controversially succeeded by his father-in-law, the Arabs had already carried the word by force of arms through much of the Arabian Peninsula. Although their warlike nature had always been known, the Arabs had been seen as little more than raiders. Now, however, their aggression was channeled by faith. Within a few decades, these desert nomads made much of the known world their own, building an Islamic empire that stretched from the edges of India to southern Spain.

Today millions of Muslims visit Mecca and circle the Kaaba. ↗

The Kaaba

Mecca was a holy place long before Muhammad was born. For centuries, Arabs had venerated the Kaaba, a shrine that held a sacred black meteorite. Muhammad made the Kaaba an object of Islamic pilgrimage. To this day, all Muslims are expected at some stage in their lifetime to make the hajj—the journey to Mecca to walk around the Kaaba—and each summer, crowds fill the vast shrine that now surrounds it.

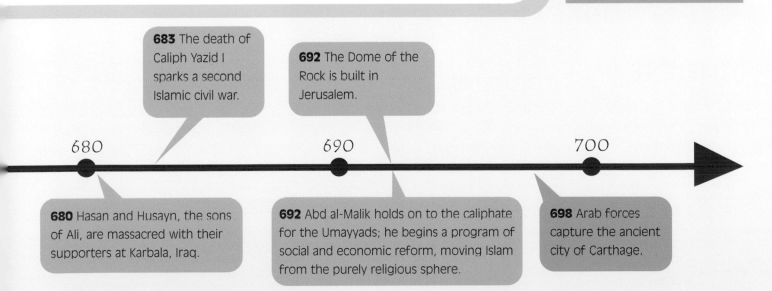

683 The death of Caliph Yazid I sparks a second Islamic civil war.

692 The Dome of the Rock is built in Jerusalem.

680

690

700

680 Hasan and Husayn, the sons of Ali, are massacred with their supporters at Karbala, Iraq.

692 Abd al-Malik holds on to the caliphate for the Umayyads; he begins a program of social and economic reform, moving Islam from the purely religious sphere.

698 Arab forces capture the ancient city of Carthage.

Sunnis and Shiites

Islam seemed to carry all before it in the seventh century, when the Arab advance appeared irresistible. Yet growing internal tensions would ultimately split the Muslim community.

The Dome of the Rock in Jerusalem was built by the city's Arab rulers in 692. →

TIMELINE
700–750

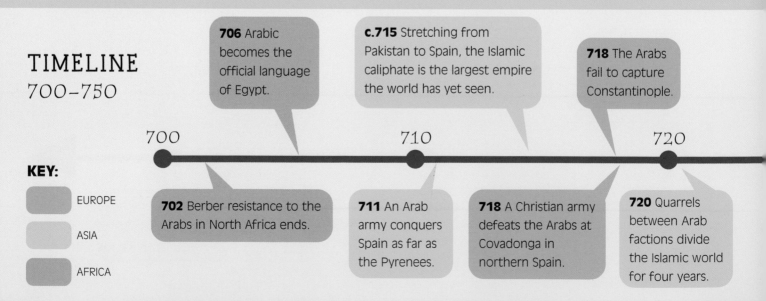

706 Arabic becomes the official language of Egypt.

c.715 Stretching from Pakistan to Spain, the Islamic caliphate is the largest empire the world has yet seen.

718 The Arabs fail to capture Constantinople.

700   710   720

KEY:

EUROPE

ASIA

AFRICA

702 Berber resistance to the Arabs in North Africa ends.

711 An Arab army conquers Spain as far as the Pyrenees.

718 A Christian army defeats the Arabs at Covadonga in northern Spain.

720 Quarrels between Arab factions divide the Islamic world for four years.

The death of the Prophet Muhammad in June 632 was a time of hope and expectation. His visions had already formed the basis of a significant religion, with followers through much of Arabia and beyond. The Prophet had led expeditions in Byzantine Syria— perhaps sensing that a military project was the best way of uniting his people's traditionally quarrelsome tribal factions.

↑ In only a short time, the great cities of west Asia came under the control of the Islamic faith.

Choosing the Prophet's Successor

But first of all, it had to be decided who was to succeed the Prophet as leader of the Muslims: Muhammad had left no son. The seeds of future division were sown when a meeting of elders chose Abu Bakr, the Prophet's father-in-law, as *khalifah*, or caliph—a title that implied both spiritual authority and political rule. This choice passed over Muhammad's cousin and son-in-law, Ali, whose

Timeline of Sunnis and Shiites

632 Muhammad dies; Abu Bakr, his father-in-law, follows him as first of the *Rashidun*, or "rightly guided" caliphs.

656 The Prophet's son-in-law Ali becomes caliph; civil war breaks out between Ali and Muawiya, governor of Syria.

661 The war ends with Ali's murder. Muawiya's Umayyad dynasty rules the Islamic world for 90 years.

680 Husayn, son of Ali, tries to seize power from Muawiya's heir, Yazid, but is killed.

683 Abd al-Malik becomes caliph; he permanently alienates Shiites.

711 Muslims raid southern Spain.

← The Arabs made beautiful but practical objects for nomadic life.

739 The Kharijite sect of Muslims rises against Arab rule in Morocco.

749 The rebels proclaim as caliph Abu al-Abbas, a member of the Abbasid family descended from the Prophet's uncle, Abbas.

730

740

750

732 At Tours, deep inside France, a Frankish army led by Charles Martel defeats an Arab army from Spain, halting the advance of Islam in Europe.

747 In Khorasan, Iran, a rebellion begins among converts to Islam who do not enjoy the same tax privileges as Arabs.

750 The Abbasids overthrow the last Umayyad caliph at the Battle of the Zab and kill most of the Umayyad family.

Timeline (continued)

715 The Arabs conquer Spain and Portugal.

732 The Arab advance in Europe is stopped at Tours in France.

750 The Umayyads are overthrown by the Abbasids. The last Umayyads move to southern Spain.

913 Abbasid power suffers when Persia is overrun by Buyids from the Caspian Sea.

945 The Buyids conquer Iraq, the heartland of Abbasid rule.

969 A North African tribe, the Fatimids, seize power in Egypt on their way to a wider dominance in the Islamic world.

← The Umayyad Mosque was built in Damascus, Syria, in the eighth century.

moral rigidity and religious fervor may have made the elders wary.

In a series of civil wars fought over the next 53 years, first Ali and then his sons attempted to take back the succession that they saw as rightly theirs. Over time, differences in belief would further separate the rival groups. Those who followed Abu Bakr and the succession of "rightly guided" caliphs who

The Umayyad Mosque was built on a huge scale. ⟶

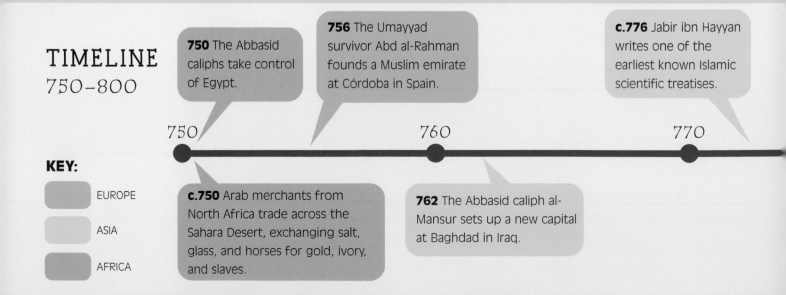

TIMELINE 750–800

750 The Abbasid caliphs take control of Egypt.

756 The Umayyad survivor Abd al-Rahman founds a Muslim emirate at Córdoba in Spain.

c.776 Jabir ibn Hayyan writes one of the earliest known Islamic scientific treatises.

750   760   770

c.750 Arab merchants from North Africa trade across the Sahara Desert, exchanging salt, glass, and horses for gold, ivory, and slaves.

762 The Abbasid caliph al-Mansur sets up a new capital at Baghdad in Iraq.

KEY:

EUROPE

ASIA

AFRICA

came after him called themselves Sunni Muslims, because they followed the *sunnah,* or "customs," established by the Prophet. Shiites argued that this succession had been corrupted at the start and that Islamic tradition should have flowed directly through Ali to the imams, or "teachers," who came after him.

Shiites and Sunnis

In 680, Ali's son Husayn and a small band of followers were killed near Karbala in what is now Iraq as they traveled to join rebels in Iran who supported his claim to the caliphate. The deaths gave Shiism its first martyrs and lent the movement a new impetus. By 750, the Sunnis of the Umayyad Dynasty had been swept away by the Abbasid caliphs, based in Baghdad. Although this was not strictly a Shiite revolution—Shiism recognized no rule higher than that of its imams—the Abbasids could not have succeeded without the backing of the Shiite scholars. Divisions between Sunni and Shia Islam have lasted to this day, a source of distrust and at times open warfare.

A Shiite Shrine

Some 80 miles (130 km) from Baghdad, Iraq, stands Mashad Gharwah, said to be the burial place of Ali, Muhammad's son-in-law. It is one of the holiest shrines of Shia Islam. Its importance can be judged by the fact that visiting Najaf and Karbala (where Ali's sons Hasan and Husayn lie buried) is seen as spiritually equivalent to the hajj, or pilgrimage to Mecca.

↑ A delicate screen covers a window in the Mashad Gharwah.

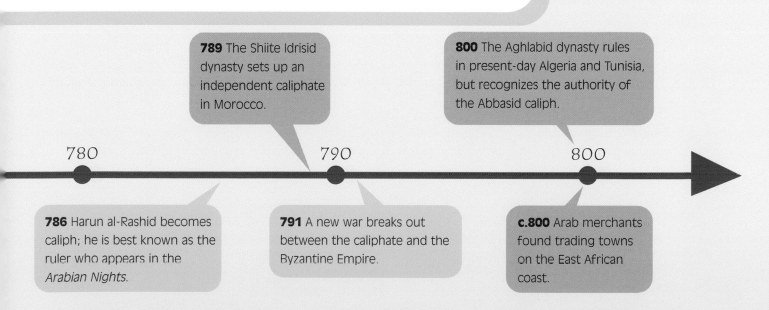

789 The Shiite Idrisid dynasty sets up an independent caliphate in Morocco.

800 The Aghlabid dynasty rules in present-day Algeria and Tunisia, but recognizes the authority of the Abbasid caliph.

780   790   800

786 Harun al-Rashid becomes caliph; he is best known as the ruler who appears in the *Arabian Nights.*

791 A new war breaks out between the caliphate and the Byzantine Empire.

c.800 Arab merchants found trading towns on the East African coast.

The Seljuk Turks

In 1071, a Muslim army captured the Byzantine emperor in a battle at Manzikert in eastern Anatolia. The victors were not Arabs but a Turkic dynasty called the Seljuks.

The Mausoleum of Ulugh Beg Miranshah stands in Ghazni, Afghanistan. ⇒

TIMELINE
800–850

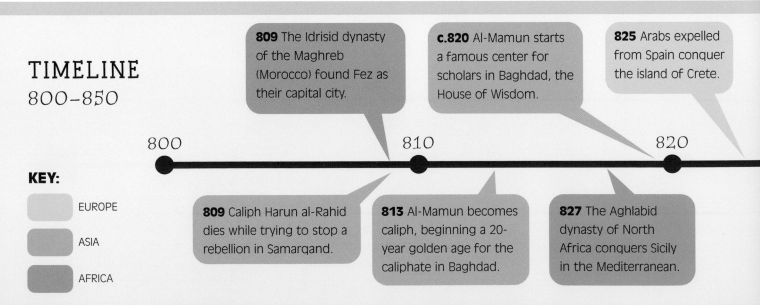

809 The Idrisid dynasty of the Maghreb (Morocco) found Fez as their capital city.

c.820 Al-Mamun starts a famous center for scholars in Baghdad, the House of Wisdom.

825 Arabs expelled from Spain conquer the island of Crete.

800

810

820

KEY:

EUROPE

ASIA

AFRICA

809 Caliph Harun al-Rahid dies while trying to stop a rebellion in Samarqand.

813 Al-Mamun becomes caliph, beginning a 20-year golden age for the caliphate in Baghdad.

827 The Aghlabid dynasty of North Africa conquers Sicily in the Mediterranean.

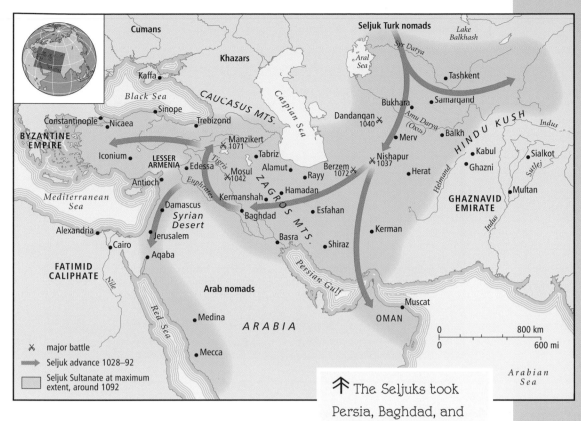

⤒ The Seljuks took Persia, Baghdad, and later the Byzantine Empire in Turkey.

Seljuk, the founder of the dynasty, came from a Turkic tribe originally from Mongolia. Early in the eleventh century, having converted to the Sunni branch of Islam, the Seljuks moved into Khurasan, a Persian region controlled by the Afghan ruler Mahmud of Ghazni. The Seljuks wreaked so much havoc that Mahmud eventually drove them back across the Oxus River.

Timeline of the Seljuk Turks

c.1010 Date of the death of Seljuk; he is succeeded by his son Arslan ("Lion").

c.1020 The Seljuks are border mercenaries in Transoxiana, the land beyond the Oxus River.

1029 Mahmud of Ghazni drives the Seljuks out of Khurasan (northeastern Iran).

1035 The Seljuks return to Khurasan.

1040 The Seljuks defeat a Ghaznavid army.

1055 Tughril-Beg restores the power of the Abbasid (Sunni) caliphs in Baghdad and is given the title of sultan.

1063 Tughril-Beg dies without an heir. His nephew, Alp Arslan, becomes sultan after defeating rivals for the throne.

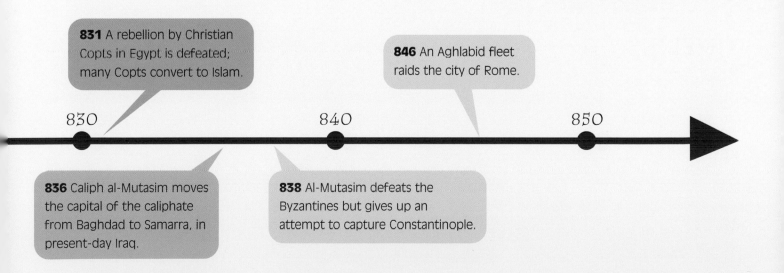

831 A rebellion by Christian Copts in Egypt is defeated; many Copts convert to Islam.

846 An Aghlabid fleet raids the city of Rome.

830

840

850

836 Caliph al-Mutasim moves the capital of the caliphate from Baghdad to Samarra, in present-day Iraq.

838 Al-Mutasim defeats the Byzantines but gives up an attempt to capture Constantinople.

Timeline (continued)

1067 The Seljuk vizier Nizam al-Mulk founds the Nizamiya madrasa (college) at Baghdad.

1071 Alp Arslan sets out to invade Egypt but turns back to defeat a Byzantine army led by the Emperor Romanus at the Battle of Manzikert in eastern Anatolia.

1072 On campaign in Central Asia, Alp Arslan is stabbed to death by a prisoner; he is succeeded by his 18-year-old son, Malik Shah.

1079 Under Seljuk patronage, Omar Khayyam and a team of scientists create what is the world's most accurate calendar for 500 years.

1090 The Shiite Assassin sect seizes the fortress of Alamut in the Elburz Mountains.

1092 Assassins murder Nizam al-Mulk. In the same year, Malik Shah dies.

The Seljuks built these towers as tombs in Iran in the eleventh century. →

Champions of Sunni Islam

After Mahmud's death, the Seljuks returned under two brothers named Chaghri-Beg and Tughril-Beg. In 1037, they captured Nishapur, the capital of Khurasan. Three years later, they smashed a Ghaznavid army.

Tughril-Beg moved west. After campaigning against Byzantine Armenia, he marched on Baghdad, whose Sunni caliphs had become puppets of the Shiite Buyid Dynasty. Declaring himself the champion of Sunni Islam, Tughril-Beg drove the Shiites out of Baghdad and was awarded the title of sultan—"holder of authority."

TIMELINE
850–900

868 The independent Tulunid dynasty is founded in Egypt.

873 Muhammad al-Mahdi, twelfth imam of the Shiite Imami sect, disappears; his followers still expect him to return and lead them.

850   860   870

KEY:

EUROPE

ASIA

AFRICA

861 Caliph al-Muttawahil is assassinated by his Turkish bodyguards, who hold the real power in the Abbasid caliphate.

862 The Karaouine Mosque is built in Fez.

871 The Safavid dynasty of southeast Iran and Pakistan establish independence from the Abbasid caliphate.

The Empire at Its Peak

Under Alp Arslan ("Heroic Lion"), the Seljuk realms were a unified empire. The chief minister was the Persian vizier Nizam al-Mulk, who filled official posts with graduates of new colleges called madrasas.

In 1071, Alp Arslan marched on Egypt, but the Byzantine emperor Romanus had set out to recover Armenia. Alp Arslan met the Byzantines near Manzikert in eastern Turkey. The battle ended with the Byzantine army in tatters and Romanus a prisoner.

Alp Arslan was followed by his 18-year-old son, Malik Shah. A member of the ruling dynasty carved out the Sultanate of Rum (named in memory of ancient Rome) in Asia Minor. Malik Shah regained some of Rum and won much of Syria, marking the high point of Seljuk rule. After he and Nizam al-Mulk both died in 1092, the empire broke into principalities. Rum survived crusader assaults and finally fell to the Mongols in the 13th century.

The Assassins

Persecuted by the Sunni Seljuks, Shiites found a champion in Hasan-i Sabbah. Hasan built up an army of fanatical disciples. These Assassins aimed to murder their targets in public places, such as mosques. In 1092, the Assassins struck a lethal blow when they killed the Seljuk vizier Nizam al-Mulk. After his murder, an Arab historian reported that the Seljuk state "disintegrated."

⇐ The Seljuks built madrasas, like this one in Sivas, Turkey, to educate officials.

876 The Tulunid rulers of Egypt build a hospital and the Ibn Tulun Mosque in Cairo.

c.900 The Persian scholar al-Razi, known in the West as Rhazes, first classifies all matter as animal, vegetable, or mineral.

880   890   900

c.890 The Arab astronomer al-Battani calculates the precise length of the year.

The Crusades

Between 1095 and 1291, armies from Europe fought wars known as crusades to recapture Palestine from Muslim control and to protect the holy places of Christianity.

Crusaders fight Muslim soldiers in this fifteenth-century painting. →

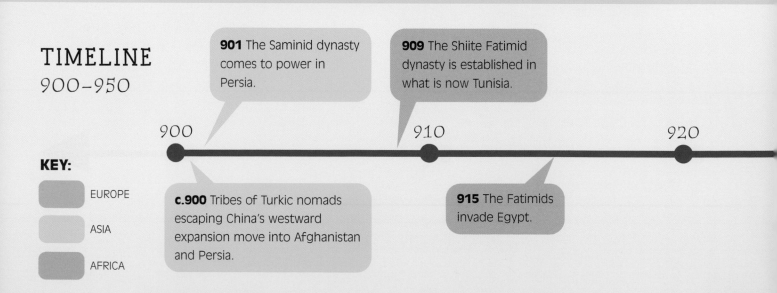

TIMELINE
900–950

901 The Saminid dynasty comes to power in Persia.

909 The Shiite Fatimid dynasty is established in what is now Tunisia.

900

910

920

c.900 Tribes of Turkic nomads escaping China's westward expansion move into Afghanistan and Persia.

915 The Fatimids invade Egypt.

KEY:

EUROPE

ASIA

AFRICA

Pope Urban II launched the First Crusade in 1095 to answer an appeal from the Byzantine Emperor for help against the Seljuk Turks, who had overrun Anatolia and Syria. An army of mainly French and Norman knights fought its way to Jerusalem, which it took in 1099.

One reason for the crusaders'

⇑ In this scene from a thirteenth-century manuscript, mounted European knights confront Muslims.

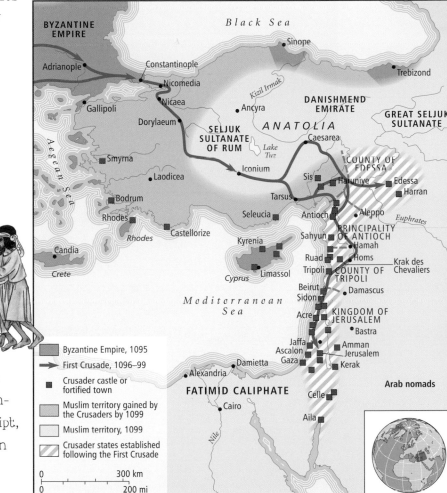

Byzantine Empire, 1095
First Crusade, 1096–99
■ Crusader castle or fortified town
Muslim territory gained by the Crusaders by 1099
Muslim territory, 1099
Crusader states established following the First Crusade

0   300 km
0   200 mi

Timeline of the Crusades

1095 Pope Urban II launches the First Crusade.

1096 The First Crusade ends with the capture of Jerusalem.

1147 The Second Crusade ends in failure.

1187 Saladin defeats a crusader army at the Battle of Hattin and recaptures Jerusalem.

1190 The Third Crusade captures Acre.

1204 The Fourth Crusade sacks Constantinople, capital of the Byzantine Empire.

⇐ The First Crusade fought its way through the Seljuk lands in Anatolia to the Holy Land.

929 Abdurrahman III, emir of Córdoba in Spain, declares himself leader of the Islamic world as caliph.

935 Arabs found the city of Algiers in what is now Algeria.

930

940

950

935 The text of the Qur'an is finalized.

945 A military group named the Buyids take power in Baghdad, where they rule in the name of the Abbasids.

Timeline (continued)

1208 Pope Innocent III begins a crusade against the Albigensians in France.

1217 The Fifth Crusade attacks Egypt but makes no real gains.

1229 The Sixth Crusade secures Jerusalem by treaty with the sultan of Egypt; it is lost again in 1244.

1230 The Teutonic Knights crusade against pagan Prussians in the Baltic region of northern Europe.

1248 The Seventh Crusade sails to Egypt.

1261 The Byzantine Empire regains Constantinople.

1291 The Mamelukes of Egypt capture Acre, the last Christian stronghold in Palestine.

Saladin, sultan of Egypt, recaptured Palestine for Islam in 1187. »

↑ This mosaic map of Jerusalem was made on the floor of a crusader church.

success was that the Seljuk Turks were weakened by internal feuds. The crusaders set up states in Palestine and Syria known as Outremer ("Overseas"). Ships from Venice and Genoa carried pilgrims and supplies to Outremer and brought goods such as silks and spices back to Europe.

The Fall of Outremer

The Muslim reconquest of Outremer began with the fall of Edessa in 1144. The Second and Third Crusades

TIMELINE 950–1000

963 The Arab astronomer al-Sufi writes a work that describes nebulae: clouds of interstellar gas and dust.

969 The Fatimids conquer Egypt and found the city of Cairo.

950   960   970

KEY:

EUROPE

ASIA

AFRICA

962 A Turkic Islamic kingdom is founded by a Turkish warrior at Ghazni in Afghanistan. The Ghaznavid dynasty will rule for 200 years.

972 The al-Azhar university opens in Cairo.

failed to halt the Muslim advance, and by 1191, the crusader enclaves had been reduced to the port of Acre on the Syrian coast.

By that time, the Byzantines resented the crusaders. The final insult came in 1204, when the Fourth Crusade sacked Constantinople and set up a Latin empire to replace the Greek-speaking Byzantine one (it lasted until 1261). There were four more crusades, but they had lost their impetus.

The crusades to the Holy Land were part of a wider movement. Christian armies gradually won back Spain and Portugal from the Muslims. The Teutonic Knights, a German and Danish crusading order, were active in converting the pagan Slavs and Balts to Christianity. And in 1208, Pope Innocent III declared a crusade against the Albigensians, followers of a heretic sect based in southern France that was violently wiped out over the next two decades.

The fortified entrance made the castle virtually impossible to take by assault. ⬇

Crusader Castles

The crusaders took castle architecture to new heights. They built massive stone structures defended with projecting towers, concentric lines of fortification, and angled entrances. The greatest of the fortresses was Krak des Chevaliers in Syria. Built on the site of an Islamic castle by the Knights Hospitalers, a military order of monks, Krak housed a garrison of more than 2,000 troops. The castle was virtually impossible to capture by siege.

977 A hospital is founded in Baghdad with 24 doctors.

984 Two Persian brothers make the first known astrolabe for navigation.

998 Mahmud of Ghazni inherits the Ghaznavid crown; he promises to carry Islam into Hindu India.

980

990

1000

c.985 Islam is penetrating the Christian kingdoms of Nubia.

Islam Comes to India

Hinduism and Buddhism were already ancient when
Islam was brought to India by invaders from the north.
Its enduring presence owed much to the Delhi sultanate.

The Quwwat al-Islam mosque was a display of the power of Islam. →→

TIMELINE
1000–1050

c.1005 The Arab scholar Ibn Sina (Avicenna) writes a medical textbook that becomes the standard work on the subject.

1008 Mahmud of Ghazni defeats a coalition of Hindu leaders in India.

1013 The Fatimid caliph al-Hakim builds the mosque named for him in Cairo.

1000

1010

1020

KEY:

EUROPE

ASIA

AFRICA

1005 A science library, the House of Knowledge, opens in Baghdad.

1008 The Persian poet Fedowsi writes the Book of Kings (Shahnama), today the national epic of Iran.

1018 Forces of Mahmud of Ghazni raid the holy Indian city of Mathura.

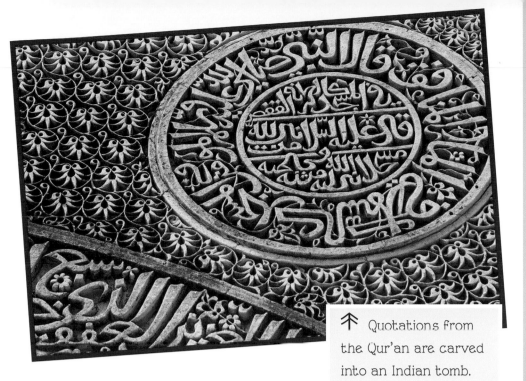

↑ Quotations from the Qur'an are carved into an Indian tomb.

711 First Arab invasion of the Indian subcontinent (Sind).

998 Mahmud of Ghazni declares jihad for the conversion of India.

1001 Ghaznavid forces first invade Sind.

1030 Mahmud of Ghazni dies; his dynasty limps on, though much weakened.

1173 Muhammad Ghuri takes power in Ghazni; within two years the Ghurids attack India.

1193 Delhi is made the center of a new sultanate.

1206 Muhammad Ghuri dies; his successor, Qutbuddin Aibak, inaugurates the "Slave dynasty."

← Islam's arrival in India brought a new style of art, as in this geometric Islamic arch.

Islam arrived on the subcontinent in 711, when the first Arab armies crossed the high Hindu Kush onto the plains of the Indus Valley. There, in the region of Sind (now part of Pakistan), they established ruling dynasties and even made converts among the native population.

No attempt at more thorough Islamization was made until 998, however. Then the Afghan Muslim ruler Mahmud of Ghazni came to power swearing jihad—Islamic holy war—for the conversion of India. By 1001, his forces were attacking in earnest. The raids went on for almost three decades, culminating in the sack of the famous Hindu

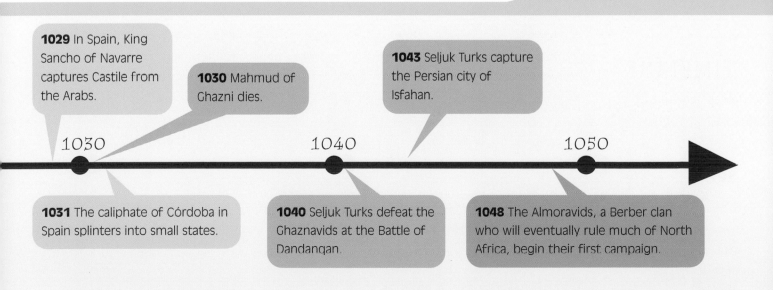

1029 In Spain, King Sancho of Navarre captures Castile from the Arabs.

1030 Mahmud of Ghazni dies.

1043 Seljuk Turks capture the Persian city of Isfahan.

1030

1040

1050

1031 The caliphate of Córdoba in Spain splinters into small states.

1040 Seljuk Turks defeat the Ghaznavids at the Battle of Dandangan.

1048 The Almoravids, a Berber clan who will eventually rule much of North Africa, begin their first campaign.

Timeline (continued)

1222 Genghis Khan's Mongols invade India but allow the Delhi sultanate to recover, although in a weakened form.

1290 The Slave dynasty is displaced by the Khaljis.

1296 Alauddin's 20-year reign brings the Delhi sultanate to its height.

1398 The Delhi sultanate is destroyed during Timur's invasion of India.

⫸ Islamic rule spread from Afghanistan to Pakistan and east to the Ganges Delta, and later to the south.

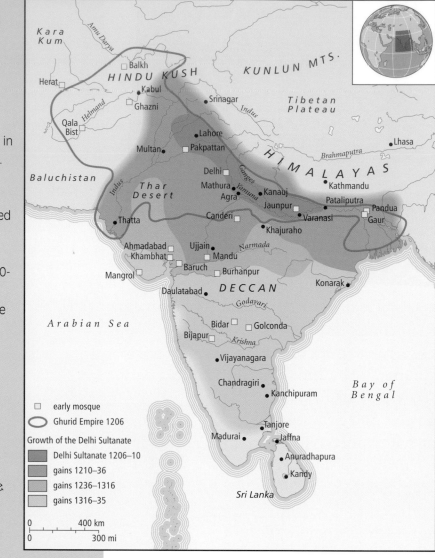

Map key:
- ☐ early mosque
- ⬭ Ghurid Empire 1206

Growth of the Delhi Sultanate
- Delhi Sultanate 1206–10
- gains 1210–36
- gains 1236–1316
- gains 1316–35

0 — 400 km
0 — 300 mi

temple-city of Somnath. By his death in 1030, Mahmud had brought the entire northern Indian province of Punjab under his own Islamic rule.

The empire Mahmud built did not long survive his death, although his Ghaznavid dynasty survived in its Afghan heartland around Ghazni. In 1173, however, it was swept away by forces of the Ghurid dynasty from the district of Ghur in eastern Iran. Originally made governor of Ghazni by his elder brother Ghiyas-ud-Din, Muhammad Ghuri emerged from his shadow

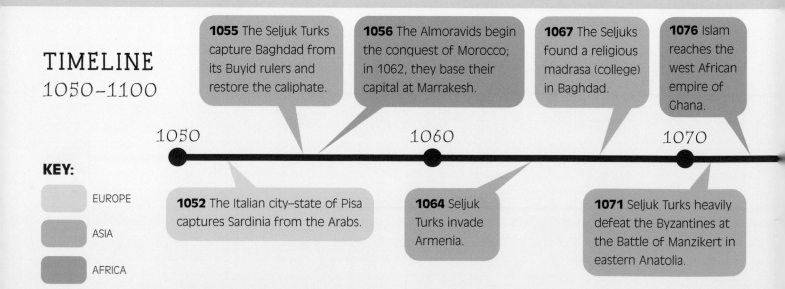

TIMELINE 1050–1100

1055 The Seljuk Turks capture Baghdad from its Buyid rulers and restore the caliphate.

1056 The Almoravids begin the conquest of Morocco; in 1062, they base their capital at Marrakesh.

1067 The Seljuks found a religious madrasa (college) in Baghdad.

1076 Islam reaches the west African empire of Ghana.

1050

1060

1070

1052 The Italian city-state of Pisa captures Sardinia from the Arabs.

1064 Seljuk Turks invade Armenia.

1071 Seljuk Turks heavily defeat the Byzantines at the Battle of Manzikert in eastern Anatolia.

KEY:
- EUROPE
- ASIA
- AFRICA

with a vengeance. From 1175, he started using Ghazni as a base for a series of raids deep into India. By 1193, his forces had captured Delhi. He went on to make the city the capital of a rich and powerful Muslim state that in time spanned the entire northern part of the subcontinent, from the Indus River through the Himalayan foothills to the Bay of Bengal.

Decline of the Sultanate

After Muhammad's death in 1206, the Delhi sultanate was taken over by one of his generals, Qutbuddin Aibak. He and several of his successors had been born slaves before achieving greatness as soldiers, thus becoming known to history as the "Slave dynasty." They were overthrown in 1290 by the sultans of the Khalji dynasty, whose most illustrious ruler, Alauddin (1296–1316), conquered much of southern India also. Yet, for all their military might, the sultans were living on borrowed time: A new and terrifying threat was looming in the north. The sultanate survived the first wave of Mongol assaults, although it was weakened. But it could not resist the invasion of Timur the Lame in 1398, which smashed the power of the Delhi sultans once and for all.

The Might of Islam

No monument shows the pride of the Delhi sultanate better than the Quwwat al-Islam ("Might of Islam") mosque. Building began in the 1190s in the aftermath of the Ghurid victory. Beside the mosque, a freestanding tower, the Qutb Minar, rises 240 ft (72.5 m) high. Built as a minaret from which the *muezzin* (crier) called Muslims to prayer, it carried a triumphant message to non-Muslims.

← The lofty Qutb Minar was a dramatic symbol of Islam's arrival.

1083 The Almoravids conquer all of North Africa west of Algiers from the Fatimids.

1086 Seljuk ruler Malik Shah drives the ruling Fatimid dynasty out of Palestine.

1095 The Byzantine emperor Alexius I appeals to the West for military help against the Seljuk Turks; Pope Urban II proclaims the First Crusade.

1080

1090

1100

1085 King Alfonso VI of Castile in Spain captures the city of Toledo from the Arabs.

1090 The Assassin sect, Shiites opposed to the Seljuk Turks, begins a murderous campaign against them.

1099 The crusaders capture Jerusalem.

Egypt's Slave Sultans

The Mamelukes started out as slaves but ended up masters of western Asia. Their dynasty controlled the region for over 200 years.

The Mamelukes' Turkic ancestors were famous for their fighting skills. ⇒

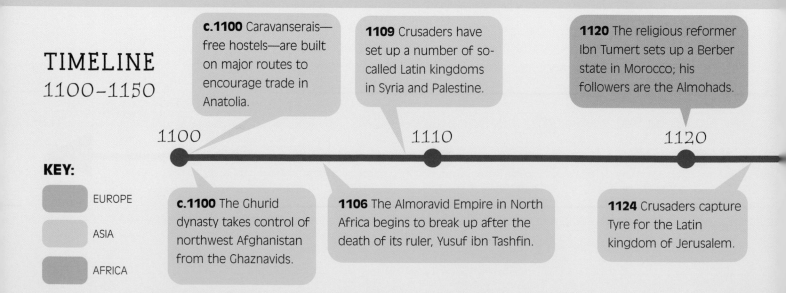

TIMELINE
1100–1150

c.1100 Caravanserais—free hostels—are built on major routes to encourage trade in Anatolia.

1109 Crusaders have set up a number of so-called Latin kingdoms in Syria and Palestine.

1120 The religious reformer Ibn Tumert sets up a Berber state in Morocco; his followers are the Almohads.

1100

1110

1120

KEY:

EUROPE

ASIA

AFRICA

c.1100 The Ghurid dynasty takes control of northwest Afghanistan from the Ghaznavids.

1106 The Almoravid Empire in North Africa begins to break up after the death of its ruler, Yusuf ibn Tashfin.

1124 Crusaders capture Tyre for the Latin kingdom of Jerusalem.

Slavery was taken for granted in the medieval Muslim world. Some slaves reached positions of great influence as scribes and public officials. Slave soldiers were particularly important. From the ninth century, the rulers of many Muslim dynasties—among them the Ayyubid sultans of Egypt—bought boys, mainly from the Turkic tribes of the western steppes, for military service. The young men, or Mamelukes ("slaves" in Arabic), were preferably old enough to have learned some of their peoples' skills in mounted combat. It was important, however, that their minds should not yet be

battle
major Mameluke trading route
Mameluke Sultanate c.1300
Mameluke tributary c.1300

0   600 km
0   400 mi

Timeline of Egypt's Mamelukes

1249 The Ayyubid sultan dies after the Seventh Crusade invades Egypt.

1250 Egyptian forces led by Mamelukes defeat the crusaders at Mansura.

1250 The Mamelukes seize power in Egypt.

1260 A Mameluke army stops the Mongols at the Battle of Ayn Jalut in Palestine, the limit of Mongol expansion in west Asia.

1260 Baybars becomes sultan, ruling for 17 years.

← Mameluke military skill allowed them to build and defend their empire.

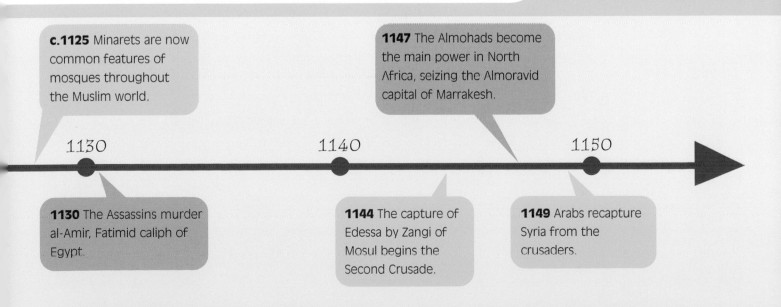

c.1125 Minarets are now common features of mosques throughout the Muslim world.

1147 The Almohads become the main power in North Africa, seizing the Almoravid capital of Marrakesh.

1130

1140

1150

1130 The Assassins murder al-Amir, Fatimid caliph of Egypt.

1144 The capture of Edessa by Zangi of Mosul begins the Second Crusade.

1149 Arabs recapture Syria from the crusaders.

Timeline (continued)

fully formed, for the other advantage of the slave soldier was his loyalty to the only lord and master he had ever really known.

Rise of the Mamelukes

When the last effective Ayyubid sultan, al-Salih Ayyub, died defending Egypt against French crusaders in 1249, his Mameluke officers fought on until the invaders were beaten. A few months later, however, they murdered al-Salih's heir and took over Egypt in their own name. The legitimate heirs of the Ayyubid dynasty and rival generals fought to carve out empires of their own in areas claimed by the Mameluke leaders.

A decade went by in factional fighting before the advance of the Mongols from the east united the Egyptians. After sacking Baghdad, in modern-day Iraq, in 1258, the Mongols paused. In 1260, they began pushing into Syria in the east of the Mameluke Empire.

↑ This iron helmet was worn by a Mameluke warrior.

Halting the Mongol Advance

At Ayn Jalut, in Palestine, the Mongols were halted by a Mameluke army skilled at the same sort of warfare as

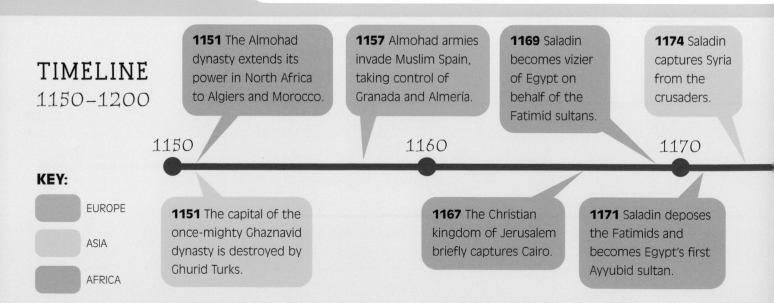

TIMELINE
1150–1200

1151 The Almohad dynasty extends its power in North Africa to Algiers and Morocco.

1157 Almohad armies invade Muslim Spain, taking control of Granada and Almería.

1169 Saladin becomes vizier of Egypt on behalf of the Fatimid sultans.

1174 Saladin captures Syria from the crusaders.

1150   1160   1170

KEY:

EUROPE

ASIA

AFRICA

1151 The capital of the once-mighty Ghaznavid dynasty is destroyed by Ghurid Turks.

1167 The Christian kingdom of Jerusalem briefly captures Cairo.

1171 Saladin deposes the Fatimids and becomes Egypt's first Ayyubid sultan.

themselves. Soon, however, a Mameluke general, al-Zahir Baybars (1260–1277), seized power; he ruled for 17 years, building an empire that stretched from southern Egypt to Armenia. Under his successors, al-Mansur Qalawun (1280–1290) and al-Ashraf Khalil (1290–1293), the Christians were driven out of the last crusader states in 1291.

Suspicious of Christian ambitions, the Mamelukes treated their Christian subjects harshly. In other respects, however, they were relatively enlightened rulers. This first Turkish Bahri dynasty declined through the fourteenth century. In 1382, it suffered a Mameluke coup of its own: The slave-soldiers who formed the new Burji dynasty were not Turkic in origin like their predecessors but Circassians from the Caucasus Mountain region between the Black and Caspian seas.

The mosque is Cairo's best-preserved Mameluke building. ⬇

The Mosque of al-Nasir Muhammad

Egypt's capital, Cairo, reached a peak under Sultan al-Nasir Muhammad, when the Mameluke Empire was at its height. Cairo more than doubled in size during his reign. In a typical Mameluke way, Muhammad proclaimed the might of his dynasty and of Islam through public works. The al-Nasir Muhammad Mosque was designed as the center of a revamped citadel.

1180 Caliph al-Nasir tries to restore the authority of the Abbasid dynasty.

1186 Forces of the Ghurid dynasty occupy Punjab, creating a Muslim power base in northern India.

1194 Khwarazmian Turks assassinate the last Seljuk sultan, Tughril.

1180

1190

1200

1184 Yaqub al-Mansur becomes caliph in North Africa; his reign is the highpoint of Almohad power.

1187 Saladin defeats the crusaders at the Battle of Hattin.

1193 Ghurid forces take Delhi, bringing Islam into central India.

Arabic Science

From about A.D. 750, science flourished under the Abbasid caliphs. Drawing on ancient texts, early scholars collected an immense body of scientific knowledge, to which they added their own important discoveries.

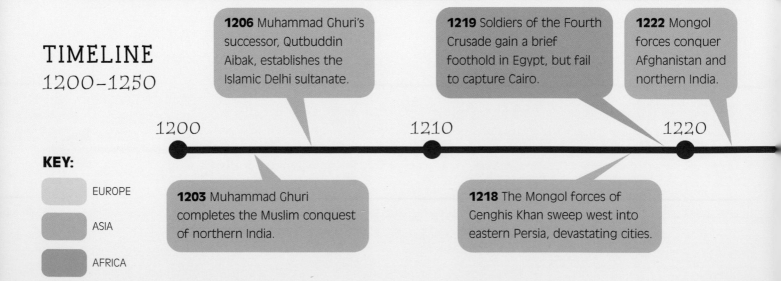

Arab scholar al-Khwarizmi introduced Indian numerals—and algebra. →

TIMELINE 1200–1250

1206 Muhammad Ghuri's successor, Qutbuddin Aibak, establishes the Islamic Delhi sultanate.

1219 Soldiers of the Fourth Crusade gain a brief foothold in Egypt, but fail to capture Cairo.

1222 Mongol forces conquer Afghanistan and northern India.

1200   1210   1220

1203 Muhammad Ghuri completes the Muslim conquest of northern India.

1218 The Mongol forces of Genghis Khan sweep west into eastern Persia, devastating cities.

KEY:

EUROPE

ASIA

AFRICA

↑ This constellation appeared in an Arab book on astronomy.

Timeline of Arabic Science

750 Umayyad dynasty overthrown; capital moves from Damascus to Baghdad under Abassid caliphs.

c.776 Jabir ibn Hayyan writes one of the earliest known Islamic scientific treatises.

c.820 *Bayt al-Hilkma* (The House of Wisdom) is set up in Baghdad by Sultan al-Mamun.

c.830 Hindu numerals are introduced by al-Khwarizmi.

c.860 Medicine is practiced in Baghdad according to the principles of Hippocrates.

c.880 Al-Battani (Albategnius) calculates the length of the year and the times of the equinoxes.

c.900 Plaster of paris is used to support fractured bones.

c.977 A hospital opens in Baghdad.

In about 820, the Abbasid caliph Abdallah al-Mamun set up an astronomical observatory in Baghdad as part of the House of Wisdom. His geometers calculated the circumference and radius of Earth as about 24,000 miles (38,616 km) and 4,030 miles (6,500 km). The correct values are 24,875 miles (40,030 km) and 3,959 miles (6,371 km).

Meanwhile, Arabian alchemist Abu Musa Jabir Ibn-Hayyan (c.721–815), known later as Geber, expanded the Greek idea that all matter is made from four

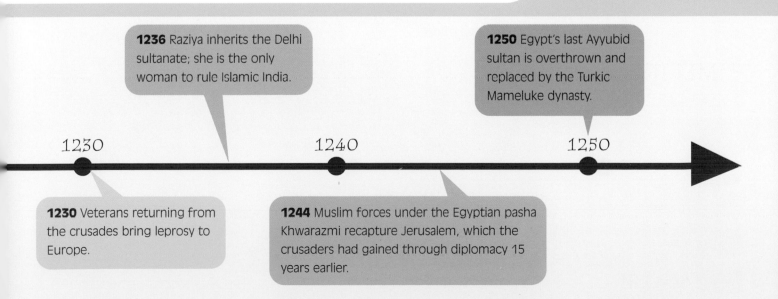

1236 Raziya inherits the Delhi sultanate; she is the only woman to rule Islamic India.

1250 Egypt's last Ayyubid sultan is overthrown and replaced by the Turkic Mameluke dynasty.

1230

1240

1250

1230 Veterans returning from the crusades bring leprosy to Europe.

1244 Muslim forces under the Egyptian pasha Khwarazmi recapture Jerusalem, which the crusaders had gained through diplomacy 15 years earlier.

An Ancient Legacy

Arab astronomers preserved the ideas of the ancient Greek Ptolemy (c.100–c.170 A.D.). The Greek's many admirers often called his main book *Megiste* (greatest), and when a Jewish astronomer and physician, translated it into Arabic in about 827, he used the Arabic al ("the") to make the title Almagest, by which the work has been known ever since.

Arabs passed on the works of Ptolemy to medieval Europe. →

elements: earth, air, fire, and water. Geber believed that the Greek elements combine to form sulfur and mercury. These two substances could be combined to make any metal, including gold, with the help of a substance called al-iksir, from which we derive our word "elixir."

Rhazes was the first physician to describe using a cast to set a broken limb. →→

Islamic Medicine

Abu-Bakr Muhammad ibn-Zakariya al-Rhazi (c.865–923), or Rhazes, became chief physician at the main hospital in Baghdad and is thought to have been the first person to make a clear distinction between measles and smallpox. He was also an alchemist. Rhazes prepared plaster of paris and described its use for making casts to hold broken limbs in place. He was possibly the first person to classify all substances as being animal, vegetable, or mineral.

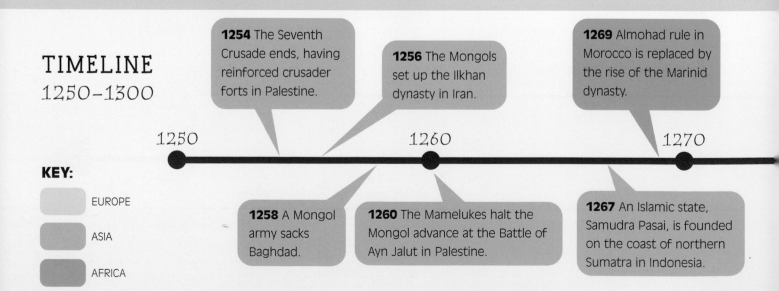

TIMELINE
1250–1300

1254 The Seventh Crusade ends, having reinforced crusader forts in Palestine.

1256 The Mongols set up the Ilkhan dynasty in Iran.

1269 Almohad rule in Morocco is replaced by the rise of the Marinid dynasty.

1250   1260   1270

KEY:

EUROPE

ASIA

AFRICA

1258 A Mongol army sacks Baghdad.

1260 The Mamelukes halt the Mongol advance at the Battle of Ayn Jalut in Palestine.

1267 An Islamic state, Samudra Pasai, is founded on the coast of northern Sumatra in Indonesia.

Islamic Astronomers

Most astronomers accepted the work of the ancient Greek Ptolemy, but in about 880, Abu-Abdullah al-Battani (c.850–929), also called Albategnius, observed that the sun was not always where Ptolemy said it should be in the sky. He deduced that its position changes slowly. This allowed him to measure the length of the year more accurately. Al-Battani also perfected the techniques of spherical geometry and was the first astronomer to use a table of sines.

The Translators

The advance of Arabic science depended on scholars who translated works from Greek into Arabic. One of the greatest was a Christian living in Baghdad. Honain ben Isaac translated the works of ancient Greek physician Hippocrates; he practiced medicine according to Hippocratic principles and used methods developed by the ancient Greek physician Galen.

New Numerals

We owe our system of numerals to the Arab scholar al-Khwarizmi. He was the librarian at the House of Wisdom in Baghdad, where he studied Hindu sources. He used Hindu numerals, including zero, in his works. In about 830, al-Khwarizmi wrote an influential treatise on math. Translated into Latin, a phrase from its title gave us the word "algebra." Al-Khwarizmi's name also gave us our word "algorithm."

← Avicenna was a famous Persian scientist and physician.

1281 Osman (Uthman) establishes a power base near Bursa in Asia Minor, beginning what will become the Ottoman dynasty.

1295 Under Mahmud Ghazan, ruler of the Mongol Ilkhan state, Islam spreads widely among the Ilkhans.

1280

1290

1300

1280 Al-Mansur Qalawun becomes Egypt's Mameluke sultan.

1291 Acre, the last Latin stronghold in West Asia, falls to the Mamelukes, ending the era of crusader states.

1296 Alauddin Khalji begins his 20-year-rule, a golden age for the Delhi sultanate.

The Empire of Mali

For centuries, a series of west African states had controlled trade across the Sahara Desert. The Islamic empire of Mali was the biggest and most wealthy.

Mali grew rich from the trade caravans that crossed the Sahara Desert. →

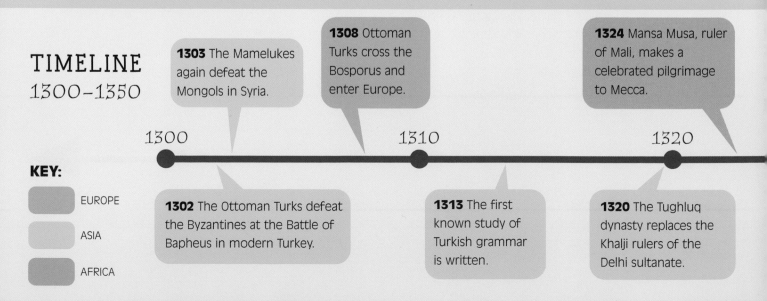

TIMELINE 1300–1350

1303 The Mamelukes again defeat the Mongols in Syria.

1308 Ottoman Turks cross the Bosporus and enter Europe.

1324 Mansa Musa, ruler of Mali, makes a celebrated pilgrimage to Mecca.

1300

1310

1320

1302 The Ottoman Turks defeat the Byzantines at the Battle of Bapheus in modern Turkey.

1313 The first known study of Turkish grammar is written.

1320 The Tughluq dynasty replaces the Khalji rulers of the Delhi sultanate.

KEY:

EUROPE

ASIA

AFRICA

When Mali's ruler Mansa Musa passed through Cairo on his way to Mecca in 1324, an Egyptian noted, "The members of his entourage proceeded to buy so many Turkish and Ethiopian slave girls, singing girls, and clothes, that the value of the gold dinar fell by six dirhams."

Mali was hugely wealthy. It commanded the goldfields of Bambuk and Bure, in modern Guinea. It also included some of Africa's richest agricultural land.

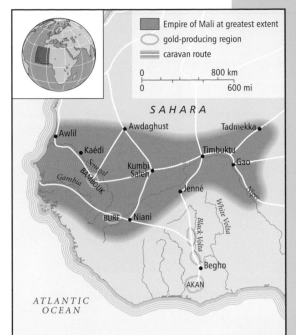

Its towns were famous for their metalwork and crafts. Upriver from the west and from the forests of the south came ivory as well as slaves. Away to the north, meanwhile, camel columns up to 30 miles (50 km) long used ancient trails across the Sahara Desert. The Empire of Mali

← A west African Muslim writes out verses from the Qur'an.

← Mali's rise was based on agriculture, gold, and trade with the Islamic states of North Africa.

Timeline of Mali

c.1235 Sundiata Keita, founder of the Empire of Mali, overcomes Sumanguru, ruler of the Soso.

c.1260 Sundiata dies after a 25-year reign.

c.1312 King Abubakar II sails off into the Atlantic; when he fails to return, Mansa Musa assumes power.

1320 Mansa Musa's forces seize Timbuktu from the Tuareg.

1324 Mansa Musa goes on a pilgrimage to Mecca. The wealth of his entourage helps draw Mali to the attention of the wider world.

1331 The Arab traveler Ibn Battuta vists the city-states of Africa's east coast.

1346 The Byzantine emperor gives his daughter in marriage to the Ottoman sultan Orhan in return for military aid.

1330

1340

1350

1333 Caliph Yusuf I brings Arabic culture in Granada, Spain, to its peak.

1333 Ottomans drive the Byzantines almost completely out of Anatolia.

1346 Muslim armies raid into Nepal, destroying Hindu temples.

Timeline (continued)

1325 Malian forces conquer Gao, extending the empire eastward.

1337 Death of Mansa Musa.

1352 The Arab traveler Ibn Battuta visits Mali, reporting that "their sultan does not permit anyone to practice oppression."

c.1370 Power passes to the tyrannical Mansa Djata at about this time.

c.1382 The death of Mansa Musa II unleashes a power struggle for the succession.

c.1400 Raids by Tuareg nomads weaken Mali.

1433 Timbuktu falls to Tuareg raiders.

c.1450 Mali is eclipsed by the growing Songhai Empire, of which it becomes a part.

⇒ The famous mud mosque at Djenne was built by Mansa Musa, emperor of Mali.

controlled the entire cross-Saharan trade, including the vital traffic in salt from the desert mines at Taghaza.

The empire had emerged in the eleventh century. The successor kingdoms that emerged from the collapse of the Kingdom of Ghana included Takrur, which reached a peak early in the twelfth century, and Soso. By 1235, a new power had arisen: Mande, led by Chief Sundiata Keita of the Malinke people (also known as the Mandinka). In that year, Sundiata defeated Sumanguru, the Soso king. Pronouncing himself mansa (emperor) of the region, he made his capital at Niani, near the Bure goldfield, laying the foundations of the Empire of Mali.

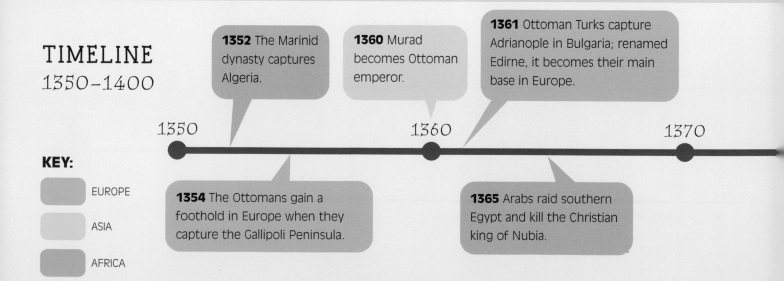

TIMELINE
1350–1400

1352 The Marinid dynasty captures Algeria.

1360 Murad becomes Ottoman emperor.

1361 Ottoman Turks capture Adrianople in Bulgaria; renamed Edirne, it becomes their main base in Europe.

1350   1360   1370

1354 The Ottomans gain a foothold in Europe when they capture the Gallipoli Peninsula.

1365 Arabs raid southern Egypt and kill the Christian king of Nubia.

KEY:

EUROPE

ASIA

AFRICA

Mansa Musa

Mali's heyday came in the fourteenth century. At its peak, its borders extended from the Atlantic eastward to the borders of modern Nigeria and from the Sahara south to the rainforests of Guinea. At the start of the century, its ruler was Abubakar II, although little is known of him except that one day he sailed off into the Atlantic with a mighty fleet. His successor, Mansa Musa, has a firmer place in the historical record: His pilgrimage aside, he built mosques in the conquered cities of Gao and Jenné. Influenced by trading contacts with the Arab world, Mali's rulers had embraced Islam in the previous century, although they encouraged their subjects to maintain traditional beliefs.

Mali declined from the early fifteenth century, assailed by raids by Tuareg nomads of the Sahara and weakened by internal division. The city of Gao on the Niger River grew in power, eclipsing its former capital as the center of the new Songhai Empire.

Timbuktu

A lonely desert oasis, Timbuktu became first a trading city then a center of learning. Endowed by Mansa Musa with a mosque and a palace, the city became the commercial hub of the Sahara. It was also the center of a vigorous cultural traffic. In the late fifteenth century, students flocked to its university to study rare manuscripts and to marvel at the city's mosques.

← The struts of African mosques are used as scaffolding during repair work.

1375 Gao secedes from Mali; it eventually becomes the powerful Islamic state of Songhai.

1380

1382 The Arab historian Ibn Khaldun becomes a professor and judge in Cairo.

1390 The Ottomans seize the last Byzantine territories in Asia Minor.

1390

1393 The Mongol leader Timur the Lame occupies Baghdad.

1396 An Ottoman army defeats European crusaders on the Danube River.

1400

Timur the Lame

The Mongol leader Timur defeated the mighty Mamelukes and Ottomans; he was also a devout Muslim who made his capital at Samarqand an oasis of culture.

Timur is buried in the Gur-i-Mir Mausoleum in Samarqand, now in Uzbekistan. →→

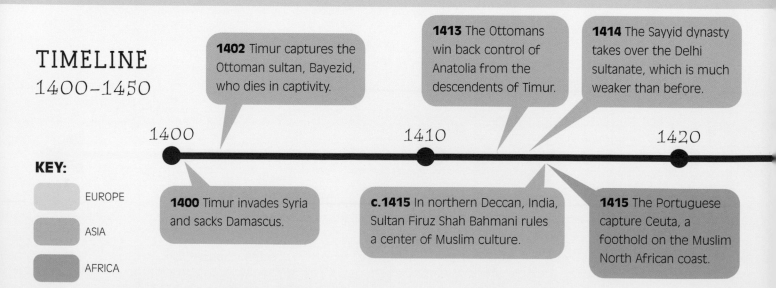

TIMELINE
1400–1450

1402 Timur captures the Ottoman sultan, Bayezid, who dies in captivity.

1413 The Ottomans win back control of Anatolia from the descendents of Timur.

1414 The Sayyid dynasty takes over the Delhi sultanate, which is much weaker than before.

1400

1410

1420

KEY:

EUROPE

ASIA

AFRICA

1400 Timur invades Syria and sacks Damascus.

c.1415 In northern Deccan, India, Sultan Firuz Shah Bahmani rules a center of Muslim culture.

1415 The Portuguese capture Ceuta, a foothold on the Muslim North African coast.

Born in about 1336 in Transoxiana—now Uzbekistan—Timur was a Mongol of the Chagatai Khanate of central Asia. An injury gave him the nickname Timur-i-Lenk, "Timur the Lame" (often shortened to "Tamberlane" or "Tamerlane"). He rose to become leader of the Chagatai by 1369.

Invasions and Massacres

Timur directed his first foreign campaign against Persia, where he established a reputation for cruelty. In 1387, he punished a revolt in Esfahan by killing tens of thousands of citizens and piling up their skulls. He committed similar atrocities wherever he went, although he was careful to spare scholars and craftsmen to rebuild his capital, Samarqand.

Soon Timur turned on two formidable opponents to the west: the Ottoman Turks and the Mamelukes of

Timur attacks Christians in Turkey in this fifteenth-century painting.

Timeline of Timur the Lame

c.1336 Timur is born at Kish, south of Samarqand.

1361 Timur is recognized as leader of the Barlas tribe of Chagatai Mongols, which rules the central Asian steppelands.

1369 Timur makes himself master of the Chagatai Khanate of Transoxiana.

1381 Timur invades Persia, which has fragmented after the death of the last Ilkhan ruler in 1335.

1392 In a period known as the "Five Years' Campaign," Timur's army devastates Georgia, seizes Baghdad for a time, and wages war on the Mongol Empire of the Golden Horde in southern Russia.

1395 Timur defeats the Golden Horde.

1398 Timur invades India and sacks Delhi.

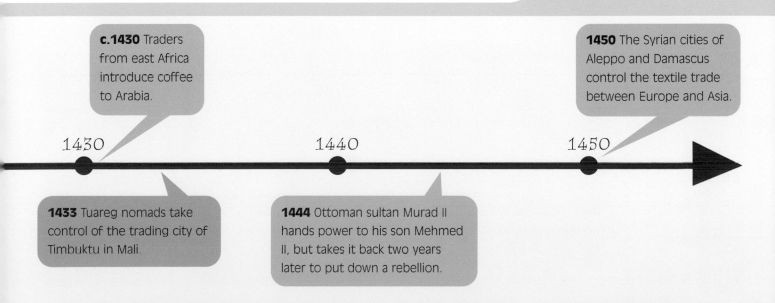

c.1430 Traders from east Africa introduce coffee to Arabia.

1450 The Syrian cities of Aleppo and Damascus control the textile trade between Europe and Asia.

1430

1440

1450

1433 Tuareg nomads take control of the trading city of Timbuktu in Mali.

1444 Ottoman sultan Murad II hands power to his son Mehmed II, but takes it back two years later to put down a rebellion.

Timeline (continued)

1400 Timur defeats the Syrian army of the Mamelukes at Aleppo; the main Mameluke army returns to Cairo.

1401 Timur captures Damascus and Baghdad.

1402 Timur defeats the Ottoman army near Ankara in present-day Turkey.

1405 Timur dies on an invasion of China. His Timurid dynasty soon collapses, but one of his descendants, Babur, will establish India's Mughal Empire in 1526.

→ Timur was notorious for his cruelty.

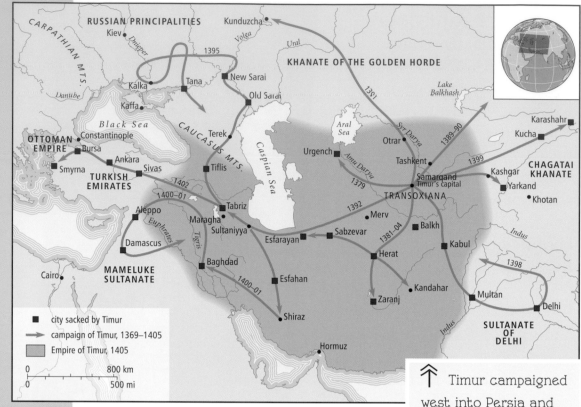

↑ Timur campaigned west into Persia and Egypt and east into the sultanate of Delhi.

■ city sacked by Timur
→ campaign of Timur, 1369–1405
▨ Empire of Timur, 1405

0   800 km
0   500 mi

Egypt and Syria. Leading an army of 300,000, Timur invaded Syria in 1400 and defeated a Mameluke army near Aleppo. On hearing the news, the main Mameluke force turned back to Egypt, leaving Timur to sack Damascus and Baghdad.

That left the Ottomans. When the two forces met near Ankara, some Turkish contingents joined the Mongols, who won easily. The Ottoman sultan was

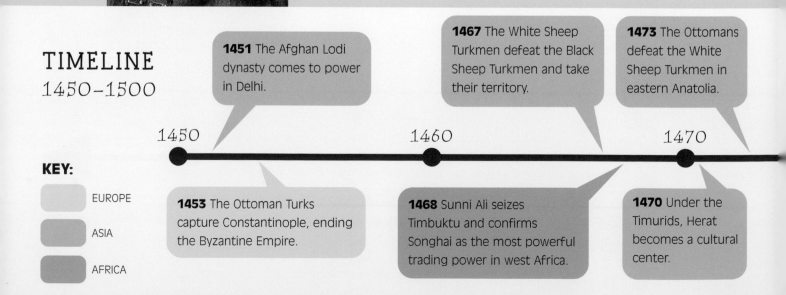

TIMELINE
1450–1500

1451 The Afghan Lodi dynasty comes to power in Delhi.

1467 The White Sheep Turkmen defeat the Black Sheep Turkmen and take their territory.

1473 The Ottomans defeat the White Sheep Turkmen in eastern Anatolia.

1450   1460   1470

KEY:

EUROPE

ASIA

AFRICA

1453 The Ottoman Turks capture Constantinople, ending the Byzantine Empire.

1468 Sunni Ali seizes Timbuktu and confirms Songhai as the most powerful trading power in west Africa.

1470 Under the Timurids, Herat becomes a cultural center.

← This star-shaped design was typical of Islamic tilework.

captured and displayed in an iron cage.

Timur now ruled the whole of Asia from India to the Mediterranean. Nearly 70 years old, he was still hungry for conquest. He set out to attack China, but fell sick and died on the way. The empire he had created soon broke up. His chief concern had always been to plunder rather than administer his territories, so he had not created a central government that could hold the empire together. Even in his own time, Timur was out of date. He was a warrior whose horseback, raiding style of warfare would soon be made completely obsolete by infantry armed with artillery.

↑ The Gur-i-Mir Mausoleum is famous for its spectacular tilework decoration.

Samarqand

The oasis town of Samarqand was destroyed in 1220 by Genghis Khan. Timur brought craftsmen from across the empire to rebuild a magnificent capital with buildings such as the Gur-i-Mir Mausoleum, crowned with a turquoise dome. Another legacy of Timur's patronage was India's Mughal school of miniature painting, which was inspired by artists deported to Samarqand from Baghdad.

1481 Bayezid II comes to the Ottoman throne; he begins a period of Ottoman expansion.

1493 The Askiya dynasty takes power in Songhai; during their reign, the Sankoré Mosque in Timbuktu is a center of Islamic learning.

1480

1490

1500

1479 The Treaty of Constantinople ends a 15-year war between the Ottoman Empire and Venice.

1492 The last Muslim state in Spain, Granada, falls to the Spanish; many Muslims are forced into exile in North Africa.

1497 The end of the White Sheep dynasty in Persia begins the rise of the Safavid dynasty.

The Ottomans

In the 1300s, Turkish armies began raiding the Byzantine Empire. They were led by the Ottomans, a dynasty that created one of the greatest Muslim empires in history.

This image shows the Ottoman defeat of Constantinople in 1453. →

TIMELINE
1500–1550

c.1500 Muslim khanates emerge centered on the oasis cities of the Silk Road.

1504 In Afghanistan, Babur leads the Mughals in a series of conquests.

1510 Shah Esmail I makes Shiite Islam the state religion of Persia.

1520 Suleiman I, "the Magnificent," becomes the Ottoman sultan.

1500   1510   1520

KEY:

EUROPE

ASIA

AFRICA

1501 Shah Esmail founds the Safavid dynasty of Persia.

1514 Ottoman and Persian armies meet at Chaldiran; victory allows the Ottomans to expand to the east.

1517 Mecca comes under Ottoman control.

1519 The Mughals begin their first invasion of India.

The early Ottomans were *ghazis*, warriors dedicated to fighting for Islam and winning converts. From a small principality in northwestern Anatolia, they made repeated attacks on the Christian Byzantine Empire, now in decline and weakened by internal disorder. The greatest of the early Ottoman sultans was Murad I (ruled 1360–1389). In 1361, he captured Adrianople, the second-most important city of

The empire grew to cover much of Anatolia and southeastern Europe. ⤓

Timeline of the Ottomans

1300 Osman I is *bey* (prince) of a region of northwest Anatolia.

1354 The Ottomans capture the Gallipoli Peninsula on the European side of the strait leading into the Bosporus.

1361 Murad II captures Adrianople and renames it Edirne.

1389 The Ottomans crush the Serbs at the Battle of Kosovo.

⤓ Sultan Mehmed II was painted by the great Venetian artist Bellini.

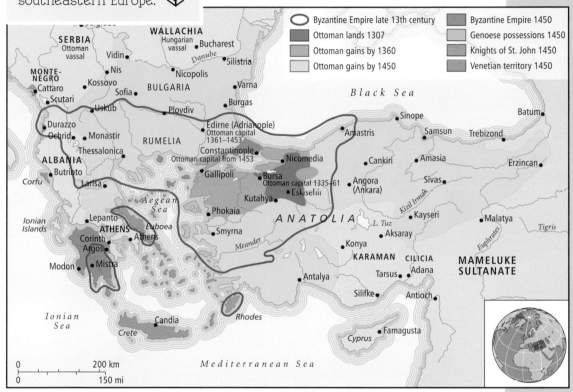

1526 The Mughals defeat the sultan of Delhi at the Battle of Panipat and take Delhi.

1534 The naval admiral Barbarossa captures Tunis for the Ottomans.

1539 The architect Sinan becomes chief of Suleiman's corps of architects.

1540 The Afghan Sher Shah Sur seizes power from the Mughals in Delhi.

1530   1540   1550

1534 Suleiman I seizes Baghdad from the Safavid Empire.

1540 Barbarossa leads a naval victory over the Holy Roman Emperor off Crete.

1542 The new Islamic state of Banten is founded on the Sunda Strait; it soon comes to dominate neighboring Hindu states.

Timeline (continued)

1402 Timur captures Sultan Bayezid at the Battle of Ankara; the empire is thrown into chaos as Bayezid's four sons contest the succession.

1448 Victory at the second Battle of Kosovo secures the Danube River as the Ottoman frontier in the Balkans.

1453 Constantinople falls to Mehmed II.

1454 Construction of the Topkapi Palace begins in Istanbul, as Constantinople is now renamed.

1473 Ottoman rule now extends throughout Anatolia, from the Euphrates River to the Black Sea coast.

The insignia of the Ottomans: Their empire lasted until 1922.

the Byzantine Empire, in present-day Bulgaria. Murad renamed the city Edirne and made it his capital. From there, he sent his armies deeper into Europe. In 1389, he was killed at the Battle of Kosovo in Serbia, which, despite his death, was a great victory for the Turks.

Ottoman Conquest in Europe

Murad's namesake and grandson, Murad II (ruled 1421–51), oversaw the next great period of Ottoman expansion. Murad ruled with the support of the highly trained janissaries, soldiers made up of Christian slaves and converts to Islam who served as his personal guard. To ensure a flow of recruits, Murad devised the *devshirme* system by which drafts of Christian youths were sent from the Balkans each year. After converting to Islam, they were given military training and joined the sultan's service for life. Although slaves, the janissaries were well treated and could rise to high positions of wealth and influence in the empire.

The devshirme system relied on conquest to produce drafts of young men, and Murad renewed campaigns in Greece, Serbia, Walachia (now southern Romania), and Albania. By now the Byzantine Empire was encircled by the Ottomans. Its fall came in 1453, when the army of

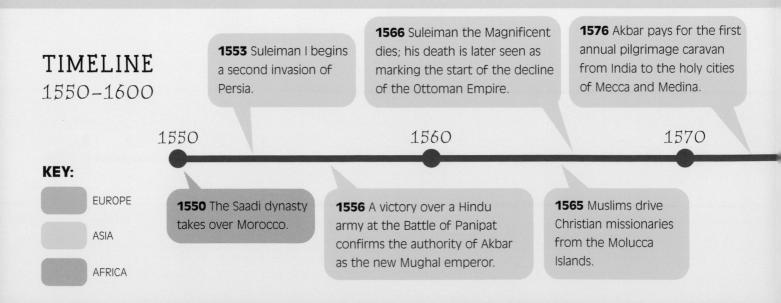

TIMELINE
1550–1600

1553 Suleiman I begins a second invasion of Persia.

1566 Suleiman the Magnificent dies; his death is later seen as marking the start of the decline of the Ottoman Empire.

1576 Akbar pays for the first annual pilgrimage caravan from India to the holy cities of Mecca and Medina.

1550   1560   1570

KEY:

EUROPE

ASIA

AFRICA

1550 The Saadi dynasty takes over Morocco.

1556 A victory over a Hindu army at the Battle of Panipat confirms the authority of Akbar as the new Mughal emperor.

1565 Muslims drive Christian missionaries from the Molucca Islands.

↑ Verses from the Qur'an appear on tiles on the wall of one of Istanbul's mosques.

the 20-year-old Sultan Mehmed II (ruled 1451–1481) stormed the walls after a siege, ending the Byzantine Empire after 1,000 years. Constantinople, now known as Istanbul, became the residence of the Ottoman sultans and the capital of their highly organized empire.

Like the Byzantine Empire, Ottoman rule proved long-lasting. It reached a peak of splendor under Suleiman the Magnificent in the sixteenth century but then fell into a long decline; by the nineteenth century, the Ottoman realm was widely known as "the sick man of Europe." The last emperor was finally deposed in 1922, in the aftermath of Turkey's defeat in World War I.

The Fall of Constantinople

The final siege of Constantinople began on April 2, 1453. The Ottomans hauled their ships overland to the harbor, the Golden Horn, to cut off the city from the sea. On May 29, their huge cannons made a hole in the city walls, and the Turks flowed in. The Greek emperor died in the fighting. The Byzantine Empire was at an end.

← The cathedral of Hagia Sophia was converted into a mosque.

1582 Akbar sets out the Din-i Ilahi (Divine Faith), which draws on elements of Islam and Indian religions.

1590 The Ottomans and the Safavids make peace; they fix their borders at the Caspian Sea.

1597 Shah Abbas moves the Persian capital to the city of Esfahan.

1580 — 1590 — 1600 →

1578 The Ottoman sultan Murad III begins a war against Safavid Persia.

1588 Abbas becomes shah of Persia; he will become the greatest of the Safavid dynasty.

1595 Akbar brings Afghanistan under Mughal control.

Glossary

caliph A successor of Muhammad as head of the Muslim community.

crusade A war or military campaign inspired by a religious purpose.

devshirme A system by which the Ottoman Empire recruited and trained slaves for government service.

dynasty A family that controls power and passes it on among its members for several generations.

hajj The pilgrimage to Mecca, which every adult Muslim who is able to do so must perform at least once in his or her life.

hijra The flight of the Prophet Muhammad and his followers from Mecca to Medina in 622, which is the start of the traditional Muslim calendar.

janissary An elite infantryman in the Ottoman Empire.

jihad A holy or "just" war, which may be waged on non-Muslims.

Kaaba A cube-shaped structure in the middle of the great mosque at Mecca.

khan A Turkic title for the ruler of a state.

madrasa A school for the teaching of theology and law, along with Arabic grammar and literature.

Mameluke A member of an elite cavalry corps in Egypt originally made up of slaves; they rose to control Egypt from 1260 to 1517.

mosque An Islamic place of worship.

nomad A person who moves around during the year in search of food or grazing for animals.

Shiites The minority group of Muslims, who believe that Ali was the rightful successor as caliph after Muhammad; Shiism was particularly popular in Persia (Iran).

sultan The usual Muslim term for a ruler.

Sunnis Followers of "Orthodox" Islam, which bases its teachings on the Koran and other holy books.

vizier An official who ran government affairs on behalf of a ruler.

Further Reading

Books

Blanchard, Anne. *Arab Science and Invention in the Golden Age.* New York: Enchanted Lion Books, 2008.

Egger, Vernan O. *History of the Muslim World (Since 1260).* Upper Saddle River, NJ: Prentice Hall, 2009.

Findley, Carter Vaughn. *The Turks in World History.* New York: Oxford University Press, 2004.

Finkel, Caroline. *Osman's Dream: The Story of the Ottoman Empire.* New York: Basic Books, 2007.

Hazleton, Lesley. *After the Prophet: The Epic Story of the Shia–Sunni Split in Islam.* New York: Doubleday, 2009.

Madden, Thomas F. *New Concise History of the Crusades.* Lanham, MD: Rowman & Littlefield Publishers, 2005.

Marozzi, Justin. *Tamerlane: Sword of Islam, Conqueror of the World.* London: Da Capo Press, 2007.

Pancella, Peggy. *Mansa Musa: Ruler of Ancient Mali.* Chicago: Heinemann Library, 2003.

Quigley, Mary. *Ancient West African Kingdoms: Ghana, Mali, and Songhai.* Chicago: Heinemann Library, 2002.

Robinson, Francis. *Islam and Muslim History in South Asia.* New York: Oxford University Press, 2004.

Rogerson, Barnaby. *The Heirs of Muhammad: Islam's First Century and the Origins of the Sunni–Shia Split.* Woodstock, NY: Overlook TP, 2008.

Tyerman, Christopher. *God's War: A New History of the Crusades.* Cambridge: Belknap Press of Harvard University Press, 2009.

Websites

http://www.albalagh.net/kids/history/
Introduction to the history of Islam

http://www.uga.edu/islam/history. html
Academic articles plotting the path of Islamic history

http://www.cyberistan.org/islamic/ muhammad.html
An in-depth biography of the Prophet Muhammad

http://www.bbc.co.uk/religion/ religions/islam/
BBC online guide to Islam (history, culture, ethics)

Index